W9-BCR-536

A WOMAN FOR ★ PRESIDENT

The Story of
VICTORIA WOODHULL

KATHLEEN KRULL

Illustrations by JANE DYER

WALKER & COMPANY   NEW YORK

To Vicky Ree — K. K.

In memory of my sister-in-law, Katie Dye — J. D.

First published in the United States of America in 2004 by Walker Publishing Company, Inc.

Published simultaneously in Canada by Fitzhenry and Whiteside, Markham, Ontario L3R 4T8

For information about permission to reproduce selections from this book, write to Permissions,
Walker & Company, 104 Fifth Avenue, New York, New York 10011

Library of Congress Cataloging-in-Publication Data
available upon request
ISBN 0-8027-8908-0 (hardcover)
ISBN 0-8027-8909-9 (reinforced)

The artist used Holbine watercolors on 140-lb. Waterford paper to create the illustrations for this book.

Book design by Maura Fadden Rosenthal/MSPACEny

Visit Walker & Company's Web site at www.walkeryoungreaders.com

Printed in Hong Kong

2 4 6 8 10 9 7 5 3 1

★ INTRODUCTION ★

"The truth is I am too many years ahead of this age."
—Victoria Woodhull (1838-1927)

There were wild women in the Wild West . . . and throughout most of history.

But the America of the mid-1800s laced itself up tight. Personal ambition in a woman was thought to be evil. Childbearing and housekeeping were her duties. No college was open to her. Respectable jobs were mostly dreary, and any wages paid to a married woman went straight to her husband. If she divorced, she could lose her children, property, and reputation.

Heavy dresses dragged her down, with waists cinched tight enough to cause serious health problems. Many male doctors believed all women were diseased and wouldn't examine them. The quieter and more sickly she was, the more attractive. A woman could not vote, serve on juries, or testify in court. No law stopped a husband or father from hitting her—though some laws spelled out how big an object could be used.

Law, medicine, business, education, religion, politics, and even fashion all reined women in. It would take someone wild to break free.

A woman named Victoria Woodhull tried.

She was born Victoria Claflin. Later she liked to recall her cheerful childhood: the pretty white cottage, flower gardens, loving relatives descended from royalty.

In real life, everyone in Homer, Ohio, wanted the Claflin family to get out of town. Their rattling shack lacked furnishings, even an outhouse. Victoria was the seventh of ten quarreling children. Their father beat them, and the boys ran away as soon as they could. At mealtimes the children roamed to other houses to beg for food.

Victoria refused to beg. But one day, when she was five years old, she knocked on a door and asked if there were any chores she could do for pay.

Rachel, the young woman who answered, let Victoria visit almost daily. She washed Victoria's hair, taught her how to read, fed her, and praised her.

After about a year, Victoria arrived to find a coffin in the house: Rachel had suddenly died. The small girl ran to the nearby apple orchard and sobbed. Hours later she felt the spirit of her friend coming to her, offering comfort.

The years after Rachel's death were very hard. Finally Victoria's father noticed her true talent: a glorious voice. When she was eight, he sent her on the road as a child preacher.

At religious revival meetings around Ohio, Victoria would perch on top of crates and call out, "Sinners, repent. Listen to me, for I know things you do not."

Her younger sister Tennessee showed unusual talents, too. Spiritualism, or the belief that the spirits of the dead can communicate, was growing in popularity. Communicating with the dead at a dollar per séance, the two girls soon supported all the other Claflins.

It was a bleak life, and Victoria dreamed of something different.

By age fourteen she was exhausted and ill. She fell in love with her doctor, Canning Woodhull. Much as she hated leaving her sister Tennessee behind, she married Canning and escaped.

But Victoria soon discovered that Canning was an alcoholic and was completely unreliable. He delivered both of her children—a son, Byron, born brain damaged, and a daughter, Zulu-Maud, who almost bled to death at birth. Victoria ended her unhappy marriage but continued to take care of Canning. She read palms, sewed clothes, acted, gave medical aid, and did whatever she could to survive and support her children.

In time, she rescued Tennessee. Traveling from town to town as fortune-tellers and healers, the two sisters were inseparable. Always Victoria noticed the hard lives of the women she met. She wondered if she could help.

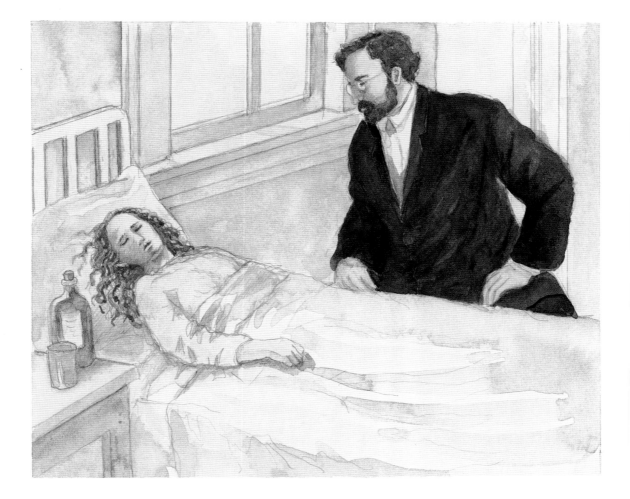

Once they hit New York City, the pair made a point of meeting Cornelius Vanderbilt, the richest man in America. Victoria put him in touch with his dead mother and offered financial advice as well. Her ways were mysterious, but Vanderbilt grew even richer.

When people asked him for his secrets, he'd laugh. "Do as I do," he'd say. "Consult the spirits." He'd reveal that a certain company's stock was "bound to go up—Mrs. Woodhull said so in a trance." He was so amused by her that one day he said he'd split the profits if her next stock tip proved right.

It did—and Victoria Woodhull was suddenly a millionaire.

Her dream of helping women took off. She and Tennessee shocked everyone by forming Woodhull, Claflin & Co., the first female-owned American company in the business of buying and selling stocks.

Every morning the sisters rode to Wall Street in a carriage with velvety red seats, white horses, and a coachman in shiny boots. Poised at walnut desks, they tucked solid-gold pens behind their ears and offered clients strawberries dipped in chocolate. Newspaper reporters went on about the sisters' gorgeous hair and clothes and sometimes commented that they "knew their business."

Men and boys blocked the sidewalks, trying to glimpse the "Bewitching Brokers," unable to believe that ladies could deal with money without constant headaches. Each night the other brokers retreated to a famous restaurant, Delmonico's, to eat and gossip.

One night after work, Tennessee and Victoria decided to join them. Inside, they sat down and ordered tomato soup for two. The waiter, instead of serving them, brought the owner, who said he couldn't possibly allow them to eat there without a man, and could he please escort them back to their carriage?

"Don't let us embarrass you," Tennessee said. She left the room and came back in with their red-coated driver.

"Tomato soup *for three*," said Victoria grandly.

At her fashionable mansion, Victoria splurged on elegant furnishings for her two children and her second husband, Colonel James Harvey Blood, who shared her interest in spiritualism and politics. Neighbors raised their eyebrows when she took in her former husband as well during his final days. Fifteen Claflins also moved in, and though they often plotted against her, her loyalty to her family never wavered.

Victoria walked at least three miles a day, stuck to a healthy diet, and never wore makeup or revealing clothing. She wanted her mind, not her appearance, to attract the attention. A witty hostess, she sparkled at parties given for the thinkers and celebrities of her day.

Wearing a trademark white rose at her throat, Victoria began speaking out at women's rights meetings. Leading suffragists admired Victoria's efforts. Susan B. Anthony hailed her as a "bright, glorious, young and strong spirit." Elizabeth Cady Stanton praised the "work for women that none of us could

have done." Isabella Beecher Hooker, sister of the author Harriet Beecher Stowe and the famous preacher Henry Ward Beecher, called Victoria "a born queen."

Women couldn't vote, but Victoria found out one day that no laws kept them out of public office. And so in 1870, she did the unthinkable. She sent this notice to the *New York Herald*: "I now announce myself as a candidate for the Presidency."

It was the wildest, most outrageous act she could dream up to prove women's equality.

Susan B. Anthony

Elizabeth Cady Stanton

Isabella Beecher Hooker

Now she had two years to build a campaign that would get people to take her seriously. She studied history to find women rulers she could learn from. She and Tennessee founded their own newspaper—*Woodhull & Claflin's Weekly*—and used it to voice Victoria's positions on the country's problems. A leading writer composed her official biography as she began the expensive process of getting her name on the ballot in each state.

Victoria realized her campaign was doomed unless women could vote for her. So on a national speaking tour a year into her campaign, she became the first woman in history to address Congress.

That day she was so tense that her face broke out in red patches. Tennessee took her hand. Then, in a low voice full of passion, Victoria listed sentences in the Constitution that she argued already *gave* women the right to vote. Congressmen were spellbound.

All the major newspapers covered Victoria's speech. President Ulysses S. Grant invited her to the White House and reportedly told her she might occupy his office someday.

During the next local election, she and Tennessee led a group of women to a polling booth.

Three inspectors stroked their beards nervously as Victoria presented her ballot. An inspector said, "I can't take it. I can't look at it." He kept repeating himself over and over, as a crowd of men gathered around, laughing.

When Victoria finally stepped aside, she was rigid with humiliation at first. Then she promptly gave a stirring speech about women's right to vote.

After the failed voting attempt, Victoria's name began coming up in sermons and at social gatherings. Newspapers tended to belittle the campaign as "entertaining." They called her women supporters as homely as "nutmeg graters." Some people even found her threatening. Harriet Beecher Stowe called her a "witch."

Harriet's sister, Catharine Beecher, tried to warn Victoria. One morning she invited herself along on a carriage ride through Central Park. No woman with "breeding" would directly challenge a man, Catharine explained—the very notion was satanic.

Victoria listened politely. Then she said, "You are misguided."

Appalled, Catharine stopped the carriage and stormed off.

Somehow, Victoria had more confidence than ever. "There was always some power impelling me onward," she said later.

By the end of her presidential campaign, she was able to finance and organize a convention for the Equal Rights Party—her most daring dream come true.

Almost seven hundred delegates, representing nearly half the states, streamed into Apollo Hall in New York City. All wanted to reform society, though all had different ideas for doing so. Newspapers called the delegates "wild men and women . . . strange-looking people." Victoria and Tennessee were the "two amazons," described, as usual, by what they wore.

At twilight, the candidate was called to the stage. Raising her arms, reaching out to the delegates, she began, "Go where we may in the land, we see inequality and injustice."

She spoke for an hour, her voice fiery, calling for revolution in business, education, politics, and private lives.

People charged forward, chanting her name.

Then she held up her hand for quiet: "Let us have justice, though the heavens fall!"

The crowd exploded. A judge from Kentucky leaped onstage to "nominate, as the choice of the Equal Rights Party for president of the United States, Victoria C. Woodhull!"

Frederick Douglass, the well-known abolitionist, was nominated as her vice president, even though he wasn't present. (He later declined the honor.)

Men shouted themselves hoarse, standing on their seats, throwing hats in the air. Women waved handkerchiefs, and some, born in poverty like their candidate, wept openly. Passersby, outside on Broadway, were startled by the commotion.

Victoria Woodhull beamed back at the crowd and savored the triumph.

Coming from nowhere, she had united a broad range of people into a new political party—to support her as the first woman candidate for president.

It was a wild moment in American history, and times would never be the same for women.

VICTORIA C. WOODHULL
CANDIDATE FOR THE
PRESIDENCY OF THE UNITED STATES